INVESTING
IS THE
NEW
COOKING

A Woman's Guide to Wealth Creation

I0491082

SAPNA NARANG

INDIA · SINGAPORE · MALAYSIA

Notion Press

Old No. 38, New No. 6
McNichols Road, Chetpet
Chennai - 600 031

First Published by Notion Press 2020
Copyright © Sapna Narang 2020
All Rights Reserved.

ISBN 978-1-64850-624-6

Contents

Introduction

*Never doubt that you are valuable
and powerful and deserving of
every chance in the world to
pursue your dreams.*

– Hillary Clinton

Do you need to take care of yourself or your family?

If yes, then you need to take care of your money, investments and wealth. The majority of women I have spoken to over the years do not give adequate importance to managing their investments, building assets, or growing their wealth. This appears to be due to our social conditioning. Growing up, we have seen papa take care of the money and mama take care of hearth. Investing is seen as a man's domain. Men in the family intuitively take over the financial role while women intuitively take over the cooking role. But today, investing is the new cooking!

Managing family investments well, is as integral to caring for the family's wellbeing, as providing nutritious meals. I have been in the financial services industry for 25 years. During this time, I have interacted with many highly educated and accomplished women who have little idea about their family investments. It is fine if our father, or husband, or uncle is taking care of the execution and management of financial matters, but it is important for us to have an overview of the financial situation. Be a part of the conversation.

Our family investments and assets act as an opportunity enabler and safety net. They provide our family with life-enhancing choices. Financial health supports emotional, mental and physical health. A strong financial foundation can provide us, and our families with numerous possibilities.

My hope is that this book will inspire you to focus on your wealth creation journey.

Best Wishes & Bon Voyage

Sapna

Chapter 1

The New Cooking

Money is not the most important thing in life, but it's reasonably close to oxygen on the 'gotta have it' side.

– Zig Ziglar

Our ancestors learnt to preserve seeds, cure meats, make cheese, bake breads, and more while living through tough times. Most of these skills were the domain of the women of the household. These were essential skills passed down from mother to daughter. These skills were learned and enhanced by the women of the household for the well-being of their families.

We do not need to be master chefs to prepare healthy and nutritious meals for our family. We have learnt cooking by observing our mothers, aunts, and maybe even our fathers. Through the generations, we have imbibed the idea, that it is our responsibility to put together a healthy meal as it is linked to the well-being of our family. Cooking is not learnt in a day. We have learnt through a process of trial and error, asking for help and guidance. It's a journey, and each one of us is at a different stage of this journey. Once we decided we needed to cook, we set off on a discovery, learning simple to more complex dishes.

Mental Block

We do not need a financial degree to manage our money and grow our wealth. We do not need to track the equity market, or to have the ability to analyse companies, to be able to grow our wealth. One can learn the basics with guidance. We just need to internalize the idea that we have to learn to take care of our money, grow money, and create wealth for the well-being of self and our families.

Today, investing is the new cooking!

I do not think that women intentionally ignore investing. I think it is more about not consciously paying attention to it, while keeping busy with day-to-day chores. Also, it's a mental block. We have grown up with the conditioning that financial matters are not our domain. This is so, even in the younger generations. They may have discussions about financial matters, but the conditioning is so strong, that planning and implementation is left to the men of the family.

I remember the case of Savita, a smart post-graduate who was working a full-time job. She had got married a few years earlier, and the family's financial situation was difficult: ailing in-laws, high medical expenses, and no alternative source of income in the family except the two salaries. I recommended her to start a small monthly savings and investment plan.

As she got increments and bonuses, she started increasing these amounts. After about four years, she had a small accumulation, made up of the capital invested and the returns on the capital. She bought a small car from the accumulated funds and continued her regular investing. She took guidance to make a financial plan and then followed it for several years to improve her financial situation, after which she was no longer living from pay check to pay check.

***

Money for Barter

I remember when my mother and other ladies in the neighbourhood would collect old clothes for months and then barter them with a door-to-door sales lady for stainless steel utensils. There would be long, drawn-out bargaining and haggling about the value of a particular sari or a child's frock before the matter was settled and the agreed-upon utensil changed hands.

Gone are those days! Imagine trying to barter on Amazon for a utensil. We no longer have access to the kinds of commodities our parents or grandparents may have used for barter. Anything and everything that we want today has to be bartered with money. Money is bartered for clothes, education, car, house, medical care, and so on. You get my point. All of our life needs and wants are linked to money.

Like we have intuitively internalised that 'cooking' is linked to the health and well-being of our families, in the same way we need to internalise that financial well-being is linked to the overall well-being of ourselves and our families.

Going forward, we women have to categorise 'investing' as a basic skill set at par with 'cooking'. Prudent investing and resultant financial wellbeing feeds into overall well- being. Investing is the new cooking!

Chapter 2

Overcome
the Mental Block

Inaction breeds doubt and fear.
Action breeds confidence and courage.
If you want to conquer fear,
do not sit at home and think about it.
Go out and get busy.

– Dale Carnegie

For centuries, men went out to earn and women tended to the hearth. Without realising it, we have been conditioned to believe that mama takes care of the hearth and papa takes care of the money.

During my 25 years in financial services, I have interacted with many highly accomplished women who defer all financial decision making to their menfolk. It is essential to overcome our mental blocks and have at least a functional understanding of the family investments. These family investments are the enablers for our family's needs and wants. Thus, we women must have at least a functional understanding of the family investments. Today, taking care of the investments and wealth-creation process, must be seen as an integral part of taking care of our homes.

We do not need to be a post-graduate in finance or a CNBC addict to build wealth. If one has a basic education, manages a household, works at an office, or takes care of young children, one has the required skillset to begin the journey to build one's wealth. Most of our near-term or long-term life goals are actually financial goals: attending a professional course, taking an overseas holiday, learning Zumba, buying a car, buying a house, educating kids, contributing to a charity, and so on. Wealth is an opportunity enabler. All one needs is the courage and will to start.

We will only reach the finish line
of achieving our financial goals
if we decide to start!

Take the case of young Amrita, a 27-year-old post graduate working with an MNC consultancy company, earning Rs 3 lacs per month. Even after paying for rent, lifestyle expenses, and so on, she had money accumulating in her savings. When she met me, she had a sizeable balance and was expecting a bonus in a few months.

Her lament was, "I know I need to do something with my money, but what?"

I discussed the "WHY" and "HOW" of investing with her. A calculation of what the corpus was likely to look like after five years, with monthly saving of one lac (100,000 rupees), convinced her that the seed could grow into a small tree. The projected corpus was enough of a buffer for her to consider leaving a corporate job and working as an 'independent', something that she aspired for. The addition of projected salary increments and bonuses, made the investment plan even more compelling.

Some mutual funds were selected and the required application forms completed, to allow the mutual funds to electronically debit her salary account each month. She realized the "How" was simple. She could go about her daily life and the investments would be made without her intervention.

***

Your Life Changes... Your Plan Changes

All financial plans need to be revised every few years, reflecting the changes in our lives: one has changed jobs, has had a baby; bought a house, or something else. Maybe there have been relevant changes in the economy, a slowdown or high inflation for long periods. These changes may mean that certain assumptions for making the plans would have to be re-examined.

In fact, just to continue the theme, it's like a health plan or a nutrition plan. The nutrition plan that one would follow at age 35 would be different from the plan one would follow at age 45. Once you have a check-up, you may suddenly realize that cholesterol levels are up, in which case you will have to make certain changes to your nutrition to take care of that. It's the same with our financial plans. As our life or investment environment changes, our financial plans too need to change.

Investing is a Learned Skill

Today in India, thousands of women have taken up jogging or running as a way to gain overall fitness. These same women may have led a sedentary lifestyle, or been overweight, or just unmotivated. With some prodding and guidance, these same women have got up to run half-marathons. There are support groups, coaches, motivators, and friends. After running the first five-kilometre race, it is a mind-set change.

It is the same with investments. I urge you to get up and take the first step. Once you have put together a small nest egg, you will be more confident in your journey. All fields have their own complexity, be it cooking, nutrition, beauty care, running, hiking, or mountaineering. In all fields, we start on a journey of learning, sometimes failing, turning to trainers for guidance, and then gradually improving our game.

Wealth creation is the same. It is a journey. All you need to do is shrug off that social conditioning, push away those mental blocks, and start!

Chapter 3

Create Assets, Create Choices

Someone is sitting in the shade today because someone planted a tree a long time ago.

– Warren Buffet

Most of us were told to study hard to get good jobs. We started earning, got the first few salaries, bought better clothes, smartphones, electronics, and enjoyed meals out. We changed jobs or got a promotion with a higher salary, and that meant more disposable income. We bought bigger stuff on credit cards or equated monthly instalments (EMIs), got married, had children, made a down payment on a house, and the list goes on and on.

It is a constant race to meet ever-growing expenses and commitments. It does not matter how much we earn. What matters is how much we spend! In most cases, the expenses grow with the salary. Once our expenses start growing as fast as our salaries, we are officially part of the rat race. We cannot get off the treadmill and God help us if the company we are working for, goes in for downsizing or rightsizing.

I remember the case of Pritam, a 50-year-old head of HR of a large corporation who was earning a seven-figure salary. She had been working for nearly 30 years and was passionate about writing. Her children were in college. All she wanted to do was get off the treadmill and write. She wanted to build a career around writing and consulting.

We put the big picture together, calculated her present net worth by considering the cost of remaining college education, projected expenses for children's marriages, outstanding future outflows for the property, etc. We then considered the likely influences of salary, bonuses, employee stock ownership plans (ESOPs), rentals, etc. After this, we calculated the retirement corpus needed to support her family's lifestyle for 30 years.

Based on the financial plan, she was able to retire at age 55 and start her writing career. The financial plan gave her a roadmap and confidence to pursue her passion. She had built assets over the years: property, financial portfolio, ESOPs, and Provident fund. She was able to get off the treadmill and follow her dreams!

***

Opportunities and Possibilities

Building a portfolio of assets gives us the choice to do what we want and exercise various possibilities: the kind of education and experiences we can facilitate for our children, the level of nutrition and health care for our families, the choice of leisure activities, and everything else in between.

Our assets, over time, give us the choice to slow down, or to get off the treadmill. Our assets can take many forms, such as financial investments,property, businesses, or even intellectual property. These assets become our earning partners. They generate passive income. Every day, we get out of bed to generate active income. If we stop working, the active income stops, but the passive income continues.

Making Money 24 Hours a Day

As opposed to the active income from working, our passive income earns money even when we are not thinking about it. Passive income is fantastic for wealth creation. After the initial outlay of time and money (such as purchasing a property), the money keeps growing. We continue to make money without investing more time or resources; in turn, this allows us to use that free time to create more money.

When we buy equity, we are buying a share of a company. Suppose Company 'A' has a million shares and you buy one share, so you become a one-millionth part owner of 'A' Company. As the company grows over the years so does the company's value and the value of your one share increases. You are richer. Another way to look at it is that every morning, hundreds and thousands of workers are getting up to work at Company 'A'. They're working to grow Company 'A', and hence, the value of your share.

Over the years, as you acquire more equity in different companies, you have many more people working to grow the value of your shares, thus growing your wealth. Even if you do not feel like getting out of bed for a few days, others are getting out of bed to make you wealthy. This is how the wealthy grow wealthier. They buy assets! Over the years the assets continue to appreciate, even as they go about their daily lives.

Many of us come from families in which our fathers worked for the government and retired with a pension. Many of us today work for private companies or are part of the gig economy. We have to provide for our own pensions, our own Social Security, and our own health care. To support all of these, we need to create assets and build wealth. A simple thumb rule is to save and invest 15% to

20% of our salaries at the start of our careers and later as per our financial plan.

When we create assets, we create our life choices!

Chapter 4

Assets and Liabilities

*Too many people spend money they haven't
earned, to buy things they don't want,
to impress people they don't like.*

– Will Rogers

Just saving does not make us rich. Investing
makes us rich. Investing is making our money
work for us. When money is invested in bonds,
equity, and real estate, it grows over time. That
money has worked to create more money.
Bonds, equity, and real estate in which money
is invested, are called assets. The golden rule
for wealth creation is to buy assets.

Understanding Assets and Liabilities

- By basic accounting definition and rules, assets are anything you buy and own.
- Liabilities are the loans, mortgages, EMI, and credit card outstanding balances that are used to buy the assets.

If you took a loan to buy a car as per accounting rules, your personal balance sheet would show the loan as a liability and the car as an asset.

- For Wealth Creation, please internalize that assets are ONLY those things which make money for you. Another way to put it is that an asset is something that is likely to grow in value over a period of time.
- From a wealth creation perspective, a car is not an asset. A car will not grow in value; even if it's a Mercedes. In fact, it is something on which you have to regularly spend for upkeep. In the book of wealth creation, it is a liability!

Instead, if you bought a mutual fund, a bond, direct equity or a company fixed deposit, you would be putting money into something that would gain in value and create returns over time. These are assets. The house you buy to live in, is not an asset. It will not generate income for you. When you need funds, you cannot sell off the third bathroom or the second balcony that you are not using. A house, car, or the latest smartphone all support your lifestyle. They are not assets for wealth creation.

Let us take the case of Raksha, 55 years old, the head of a consulting firm earning a seven-figure salary. Her family regularly took overseas holidays, kept a membership of a posh club, had a Mercedes, a Land Rover; all the trappings of a luxurious lifestyle.

Some years back, the family sold their apartment. They added to the sale proceeds and bought an apartment in an up- market complex. The move increased lifestyle expenses and apartment maintenance costs. The more up-market neighbourhood meant higher cost of keeping up with the Joneses: more expensive parties, expensive gifting, expensive outings, and so forth.

She met with me to discuss retirement planning and was shocked to realize that the sum total of her financial portfolio, projected salary increases, and bonuses were not enough for her to retire at age 60 and support her present lifestyle. Her biggest investment was her present house, which could not be used to finance her retirement if she remained living in it.

Her lifestyle had expanded along with the salary and insufficient assets had been built over the years to support such a lifestyle. She had to make the difficult decision to sell her house and downsize, to be able to have a comfortable retirement.

***

Assets Versus Liabilities

Understanding the difference between assets and liabilities is the foundation of the wealth creation journey. Let us explore these differences through a simple cash-flow diagram. Look at the diagram showing financial statement A.

- The top half, showing income and expenses, is called an Income Statement or Profit and Loss Statement. This shows where the money comes from and where the money goes.

- The bottom half is called a Balance Sheet and gives a tally of your assets and liabilities.

Now, let us understand the relationship between the two.

Financial Statement A

When you are starting out your career, you are likely to be represented by financial statement A. You earn a salary; spend it on paying your taxes, rent, and day-to-day living expenses.

FINANCIAL STATEMENT 'A'

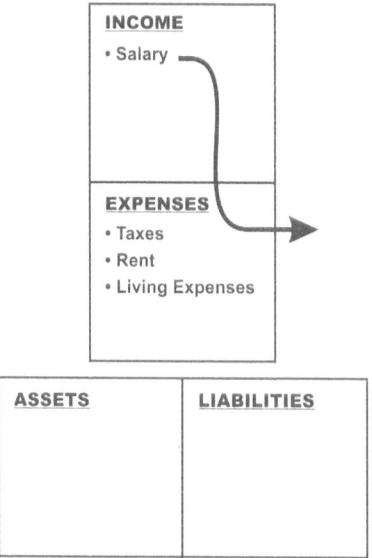

The monthly salary gets over and there is no surplus for investing. There are no assets or significant liabilities at this stage. One is living from salary to salary.

Now fast forward. A few years have passed, and you have got a salary increase. Maybe you have started a consultancy or have a small business. Your living expenses have increased. You may have got married, bought a car on loan, bought a house with a mortgage, and are using debt to finance them. You are now represented by financial statement B.

Financial Statement B

At this stage, your total income is consumed by taxes, rent, mortgage payments, and credit card debt. There may be some savings on the side. As years pass, you do well and get promotions; your salary goes up, but so do living expenses: better clothes, better electronics, better restaurants, and better holidays. You are now in a rat race. You have to earn just to keep up with the Joneses.

FINANCIAL STATEMENT 'B'

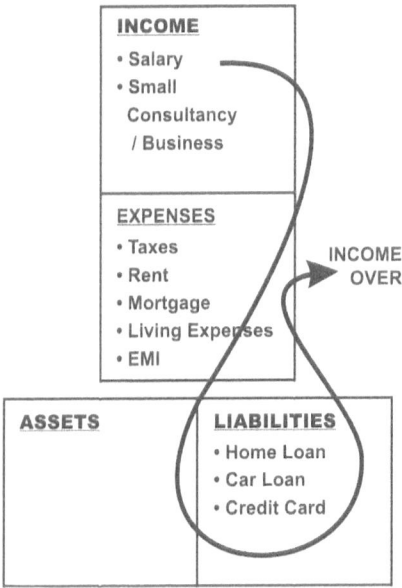

This is the stage in which vast majority of the working population is stuck. One is, in a way, tied to the treadmill. Salaries are increasing, but so are the family lifestyle aspirations. One has to run after salaries, incentives and bonuses, to meet the growing monthly EMI commitments.

By exerting financial discipline over a period of time, one can move over to a more desirable situation represented by financial statement C.

Financial Statement C

In this situation, you have built assets which generate income, which supplements income from your salary. The income from your assets could be by way of rental income, dividends from shares or mutual fund units, interest from deposits, and so on. This extra income from assets and the incremental salary or annual bonuses is used to pay off home loans, car loans, and consumer loans.

FINANCIAL STATEMENT 'C'

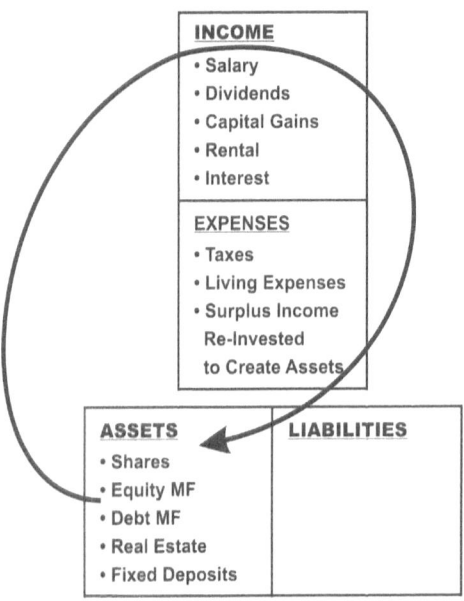

INCOME
- Salary
- Dividends
- Capital Gains
- Rental
- Interest

EXPENSES
- Taxes
- Living Expenses
- Surplus Income
  Re-Invested
  to Create Assets

ASSETS
- Shares
- Equity MF
- Debt MF
- Real Estate
- Fixed Deposits

LIABILITIES

To reach this desired situation, one needs to invest every month from every salary, diligently, for a few years. As salary increases, increase the monthly investments before you start increasing lifestyle expenses. This is the most important conscious decision that will set your trajectory for wealth creation. Increase savings and investments, before you increase lifestyle expenses. Make sure the investment cheques are debited from the salary account before you start paying the monthly expenses of rent, groceries, or school fees.

It is Possible

Just about anyone can reach this desired state represented by Financial Statement C. It does not matter how much you earn. What matters is how much you save and invest regularly over the years.

I have interacted with senior corporate executives earning seven-figure salaries who are still stuck close to stage B. This is because their lifestyles have expanded along with their salaries. They would have built assets, but the asset base is relatively small compared to the lifestyle they would like to finance for the next 25 to 30 years. Whether you are a teacher, dance instructor, lawyer, doctor, or corporate honcho, anyone can reach state C, where income from assets is supplementing day-to-day job income.

Over a period of time, your asset base and parallel income will give you the option to exercise many life choices for the family. The required basic knowledge can be sought from many sources. All you need is the discipline to invest regularly and the patience to let the assets grow.

Chapter 5

The Power
of Compounding

*Compound interest is the eighth
wonder of the world.
He who understands it, earns it.
He who doesn't, pays it.*

– Albert Einstein

You may have interacted with people who own
prime real estate. In many cases, they would
have told you that they bought it at X and
now it is 3X. Ask them the time frame of the
investment. In most cases, it would be over a
decade. Basically, they bought an asset and left
it alone for a significant period of time.

Start adding to your nest egg regularly and steadily. Then watch the wonder of compounding. It is not called the eighth wonder of the world for nothing. Not enough can be said about this amazing phenomenon.

Rs 10 lacs invested at rate of 8% becomes Rs 14.7 after 5 years and Rs 21.6 after 10 years. This is the power of compounding!

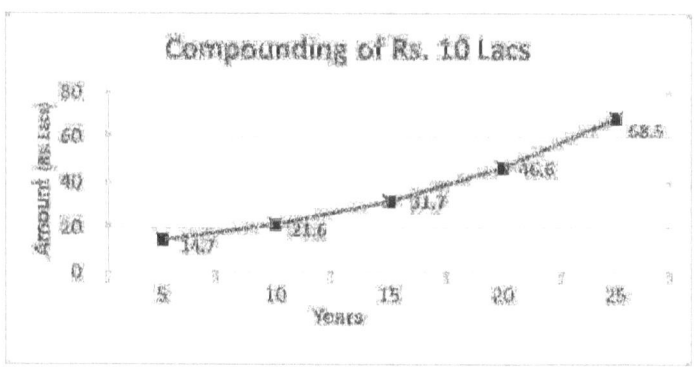

In the process of compounding every year interest is earned on interest and that is how the amount grows fast. Consider the example of Rs 100 placed at compound interest of 10% for five years. After one year the value of investments is Rs. 110. In second year the 10% interest is earned on Rs 110 and not just Rs 100. So now the investment value becomes Rs 121. In third year the 10% interest is earned on Rs 121 and so end of third year the value of investment is Rs 133.1. This is how the money multiplies with compounding.

Let me share the case of thirty-year-old, Sarita. She met me at a difficult stage of her life; she was going through a divorce. At the time, Sarita was unemployed but looking for a job. She had a 5-year old son she needed to care for. She came to me for a consult about her alimony.

Her husband was proposing a lump sum amount as a one-time settlement. Sarita's annual expenses were about Rs 24 lacs. Her husband was proposing a lump sum settlement of Rs 4 cr. He had told her that Rs 4 cr placed in a long-term deposit at the rate of 10% would give her Rs 40 lacs per annum. This would be far above her required expenses. Sarita felt that Rs 4 cr was a large amount of money and would be sufficient to meet her expenses.

I discussed with her that assuming she maintained the same standard of living, the amount of money she needed each year would be larger due to inflation. Assuming inflation of 5% per year, after 5 years she would require Rs 30.6 lacs to pay for the same things for which she was today paying Rs 24 lacs.

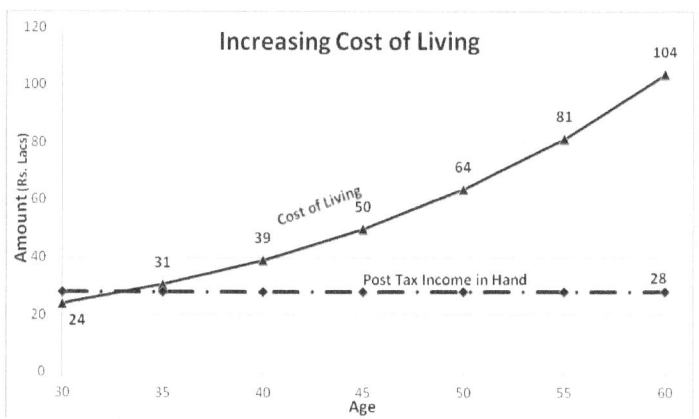

I also pointed out to her she had missed out two significant issues.

- *First: Taxes. Rs 4 cr placed at 10% would generate Rs 40 lacs. Of this approx. 30% would go to taxes, leaving her approx. Rs 28 lacs only! This would just about match her (inflation adjusted) expenses for the third year. Thereafter, the post-tax interest income would be insufficient to cover her annual expenses.*
- *Second: Her child at 5 years of age was in a nursery. But, within a few years, the child would be in primary school and his expenses*

would go up, much more than the inflation rate.

- *Considering all the facts, the post-tax annual pay out her husband suggested, would very soon be insufficient to meet her living expenses.*

***

Rate of Compounding

We have discussed earlier that in compound interest, interest is earned on interest and that is how the principal investment grows or compounds faster. If the rate (interest rate) of compounding is higher, the asset becomes bigger, faster.

This graph shows compounding of Rs 10 lacs at different rates of interest for 10 years. At a rate of 6%, Rs 10 lacs grows to Rs 17.9 lacs in 10 years. But at a rate of 10%, Rs 10 lacs grows to Rs 25.9 lacs over 10 years.

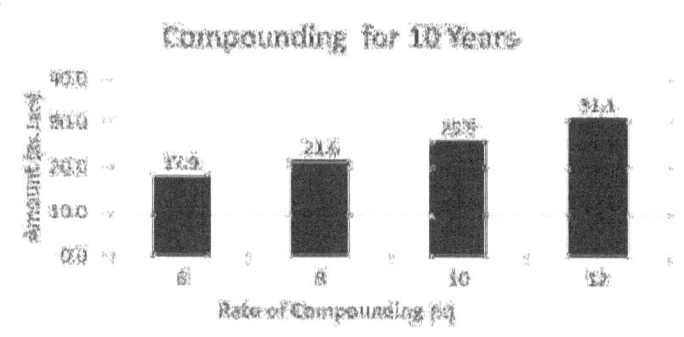

Compounding for 10 Years

The higher the rate of compounding the bigger the end result will be. That is why over longer periods of time, we can make more by investing in real estate or equity as compared to investing in fixed deposits. This is because the rate of growth or compounding, in real estate or equity, is usually higher than that of a bank fixed deposit. Also, the longer the time period for compounding, the fatter the asset grows.

This is the main reason why one should start investing early. One gets a longer period for compounding of the assets and for growing one's wealth. It helps to have a bigger asset base before one needs to dip into it, for meeting some financial goal.

Think of your assets as rabbits. You put them on an isolated island and forget about them for a few years. When you go back to the island you find they have multiplied and multiplied!

Chapter 6

Kill Debt

A budget is telling your money where to go, instead of wondering where it went.

– Dave Ramsey

Debt is the biggest obstacle to wealth creation. In fact, debt is the termite that will eat into your financial foundation if left unchecked. Debt needs to be checked and then killed at the earliest possible. Let me explain how detrimental debt can be to wealth creation.

Rule of 72

When we place money in a deposit account at an 8% interest rate, it will compound and double in nine years.

A quick and easy way to calculate the number of years needed to double money is to use the Rule of 72, which is a very commonly used mathematical rule in the financial industry. If you divide 72 by the rate of interest, in this case 8%, you get nine, so the money will double in nine years. If the rate of interest had been 10%, the money would double in 7.2 years. By simple logic, the higher the interest rate, the quicker the time in which money will double.

Debt Left Unchecked Multiplies

Assume you bought the latest smartphone for Rs One lakh by taking a loan on your credit card. Credit card loans are among the most expensive loans. Assume that your credit card company charges 20% annually. So when they give you one lac at 20%, their money will compound and double in 3.6 years (72/20 = 3.6). So, after 3.6 years, you will owe the credit card company two lacs and at the end of 7.2 years you will owe them four lacs!

This is how debt compounds and compounds. If left unchecked, it is easy to reach a situation where the interest owed is equal to or greater than the original capital borrowed.

Consider the case of young Shefali, all of 28 years, working as a mid-level executive with a corporation. After taxes, she got about Rs 80,000 net in her account. A few years earlier, a family member was in financial difficulty, so she gave Rs 40,000 from her salary and charged her own expenses to her credit card.

After a few months, the family member again needed financial support and she again gave money from her salary. She continued to charge expenses to her card. When the credit card limit was exceeded, she took out another credit card. She continued supporting her usual lifestyle expenses with credit card debt, with the hope, the loans to the relative would be repaid soon. Time passed and the interest kept compounding.

When she met me, she had five credit cards and a total outstanding credit card debt of Rs 3 lacs! Her biggest stress each month was managing her credit card bills. What she thought was a small manageable debt had grown into a terrifying monster.

***

Compounding Can Also Be the Enemy

The power of compounding works for you in the case of investments but drowns you in the case of debt.

It is a good practice to buy your smartphones, white goods or appliances from your savings rather than from credit card or consumer loans. This restraint and financial discipline is the very bedrock of wealth creation. There will be times in your life when you will need to take out a home loan. A home loan can be obtained at a much lower rate than credit card debt or consumer loans.

Before taking out a car loan or a home loan, ensure that you have the reserves to pay for several months of EMI. Once you have an outstanding loan, have a repayment plan in place. If you have an ongoing credit card debt, at the earliest opportunity, kill it!

Chapter 7

Diversify

Strength lies in differences,
not in similarities.

– Stephen Covey

Do not put all your eggs in one basket. This is an age-old piece of wisdom which never ages. Diversify your investments. There are many different types of assets in which one can invest. As discussed, an asset is anything that is likely to grow in value, over a period of time. Assets could be bank fixed deposits, company deposits, debt mutual funds, equity mutual funds, Provident fund, unit linked insurance policies, property, etc.

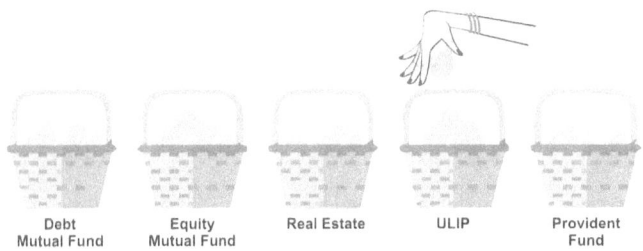

Debt Mutual Fund   Equity Mutual Fund   Real Estate   ULIP   Provident Fund

Various assets (fixed deposits, government bonds, company bonds, shares, etc.) grow at different rates and are associated with different risks. At times, the equity (or shares) could be doing very well and real estate could be going through a downturn. Also, each type of investment has its own characteristics in terms of ease of liquidity or taxation. There are different tax rates applicable on the gains made from interest or property.

Mutual Funds

A mutual fund is like a piggy bank holding the money of lots of investors. It has a professional fund manager who invests the money as per the guidelines laid down for that fund. There are many different types of mutual funds, depending on the type of investments the fund is permitted to make. A debt mutual fund would invest in bonds or debentures of various companies, government bonds, government treasury bills etc. Within this investing universe, they could be further categorised by the duration of bonds they are buying; long term or short term.

Equity mutual funds would invest in shares of different companies and could further be categorised by the market capitalisation of companies they are investing in: Large cap, mid cap or small cap.

The taxation of gains made from a debt mutual fund and equity mutual fund is different.

Real Estate

Real estate is a long term investment, usually with at least an eight or 10-year timeframe. It is an asset in which the value of the investment is locked in and will compound over a long period of time. Real estate usually requires large investment.

The advantage of this asset is that one can take a loan for funding it. The bank or housing finance company would request for a certain amount of down payment and fund the remaining part of the value through a loan. Eligibility for loan would depend on your credit worthiness, as assessed by the bank.

The taxation, loan eligibility, risk -return ratios are different for a residential property and for a commercial property.

ULIP

ULIP stands for Unit Linked Insurance Plan. I consider ULIP as a parachute for certain critical long term financial goals.

For example, my child is 2 years old. I aspire to save Rs 2 crs (at today's cost) by the time my child is 18 years to be able to fund an overseas education. I plan to save and invest diligently as per a financial plan to meet this goal. God forbid something unforeseen happens to me, the financial goal will not be met.

If I save and invest a certain amount through a ULIP, in case of an unforeseen eventuality, the insurance cover from the ULIP will fund my family to meet the financial goal. Different investment avenues support different purposes.

Provident Fund

Public Provident fund is a long term investment option backed by Government of India. This offers safety with a slightly higher return than bank fixed deposit. The plus point is that returns are fully tax exempt. Maximum of Rs 1.5 lacs is allowed to be deposited in a financial year. This scheme is for 15 years. Loans and withdrawals are permitted with some conditions.

Liquid Versus Illiquid Investments

Some investments are liquid, meaning they can be redeemed easily, and some are illiquid. If you need a few lacs to repair your house or fund a family vacation, you can sell some units of a mutual fund. You will receive the funds in your bank account within a few days. But you cannot sell a small part of a residential property. Also, it may take several months to sell a property.

Consider the case of Sunita, 45 years old, a senior manager with a multinational corporation (MNC). She had been disciplined with her saving and investing throughout her career. She stayed in an apartment which she had bought on loan and paid for. After this, she bought another residential apartment, which was rented out and the loan paid off over the years. She felt that real estate was a good way to build assets.

The loan EMI was predictable and easy to plan for. The property could be put on rent, which helped pay off the loan.

When she was close to paying off the loan on the second property, she was advised to book a commercial property, as the rental returns were higher. She booked an office and then the property market went into a downturn, and she was unable to rent out the office. While filing her income tax returns, she was informed that she would have to pay taxes on the deemed rent of the office, even though it was unoccupied.

She tried to sell the office but was not able to do it, as the property market was going through a downturn; it was a double whammy. She could not sell the property or put it on rent but, in spite of that, she had to pay taxes on deemed rent.

***

Asset Allocation

For long term wealth creation, it is important to diversify across assets. This is also called asset allocation. Different assets (Equity, Debt, Real estate, etc.) have different characteristics. Asset allocation needs to be done as per an individual's financial goals, risk tolerance and investment horizon. There is no golden formula for asset allocation. But there is definitely consensus among financial professionals that asset allocation is one of the most important decisions for investors.

Each asset follows a different growth and slump cycle depending on various domestic and international factors. It is impossible to predict and time these cycles precisely.

For long term wealth creation, follow the golden principle of diversification and remember that it is not 'timing' but 'time' in the market which makes the difference.

Chapter 8

The Fixed Deposit Myth

The more distant your financial target, the longer inflation will gnaw at the purchasing power of your money.

– Suze Orman

"Investing" is making your money work for you, not allowing it to sleep on you. Many ladies save their money and invest in bank fixed deposits, since they feel it is their hard-earned money and it should not be put at risk. They feel that fixed deposits are protecting their capital.

I see this need more pronounced in retirees. It is considered a safe bet. This is one of the biggest myths in the investing world. Investing is not about protecting your capital, but protecting the 'purchasing power' of your capital.

By placing money into bank fixed deposits over longer periods of time, one is losing the 'purchasing power' of the money. Purchasing power refers to the amount of goods or services that a certain amount of money can buy at a given time. The purchasing power of the capital decreases due to inflation (prices increase over a period of time). Suppose that today I can purchase a bag of potatoes for Rs 100. If inflation in India is 4% this year, after one year, I will require Rs 104 to buy the same bag of potatoes.

Assuming the same rate of inflation, after five years, I will require Rs 127.60 to buy the same bag. Over the years, the purchasing power of my Rs 100 will be lower and lower as the prices increase. Thus, to protect the purchasing power, our capital needs to compound at a rate higher than the inflation rate.

Pratima, 60 years old, had just retired. She had a total retirement corpus of Rs 5 cr from her Employee provident fund, savings and gratuity. She was searching for long-term deposits or bonds where she could invest and get regular return. Her annual expenses were approx. Rs 25 lacs. She had calculated that after placing her corpus in fixed deposits and paying tax, she would be able to get approx. Rs 30 lacs. She felt she had sufficient buffer in hand to cover her annual expenses of Rs 25 lacs.

We had a discussion about increase in cost of living due to inflation. She felt that the Rs 5 lacs buffer would take care of her increased cost of living for many years. To explain the huge impact of inflation on cost of living over several years, I showed her a graph.

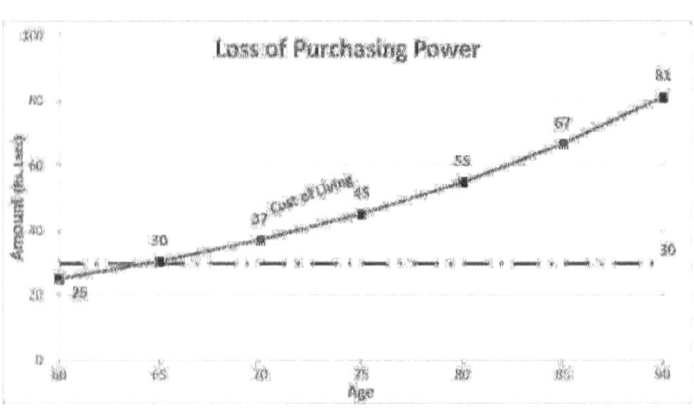

Assuming an inflation rate of 5%, her present cost of living would inflate to nearly Rs 30 lacs after 5 years. This would equal the full income in hand from her deposits. So after just five years, her living costs would be more than income from the deposits and thereafter she would not be able to maintain her present standard of living. To maintain her standard of living through a 25 to 30 year retirement, she would need to follow a different investment strategy.

***

The widening gap between the annual income and annual cost of living depicts the increasing loss of purchasing power. Wealth creation is about enhancing ones purchasing power. As life expectancy goes up, we need to plan for a 25 year to 30-year retirement. Over such a long time period, inflation will compound our cost of living significantly, thus our overall wealth needs to compound at rates higher than inflation, to keep up. The focus has to be not just on protecting the 'capital' but on protecting the 'purchasing power' of the capital.

Chapter 9

Capital Gains Tax versus Income Tax

I think if you had a capital-gains system where the long, patient capital would actually be rewarded, nanosecond capital turning would not be.

– Hillary Clinton

Different sources of income are taxed differently, leaving varying amounts of post-tax income in hand. The amount of post-tax income in hand has an impact on over all wealth. Less is the tax leakage, higher is the wealth compounding.

All Sources of Income Are Not Equal

Understanding this concept can make a difference in the compounding of our wealth over longer periods of time. Income that comes from salary, fixed deposit, interest, consultancy, book royalties, etc. is taxed under the category 'income tax'.

Gains made from selling an asset like property shares, equity, mutual funds, and debt mutual funds are taxed under 'capital gains tax'. Within capital gains tax, there is a category for long-term capital gains and a separate category for short-term capital gains. Depending upon the time period for which the asset is rolled over, long-term capital is valued more than short-term fly-by-night investments. Taxation structures help to promote this.

What Does This Mean for an Investor?

Well, all financial institutions want investors to park money in long-term investments, which can further be put to productive use. To motivate investors to do this, taxation is lower for gains made from long-term investments.

There are different tax slabs for taxing income. The table below gives the tax slab for 2019 to 2020.

Income Tax slab	Tax Rate for Individuals below 60 years
Up to Rs. 2.5 lacs	Nil
From Rs. 2,50,001 to Rs. 5,00,000	5% of the total income that is more than Rs. 2.5 lacs + 4% cess
From Rs. 5,00,001 to Rs. 10,00,000	20% of the total income that is more than Rs. 5 lacs + Rs. 12,500 + 4% cess
Income of above Rs. 10 lacs	30% of the total income that is more than Rs. 10 lacs + Rs. 1,12,500 + 4% cess

These slabs vary over the years depending on the IT rules. This illustration is just to give you an idea of the income tax rates. To simplify our discussion, I will assume that your income will get taxed at a flat rate of 30%.

Now assume that you bought a property 10 years ago. You had bought the property for Rs 1 cr and are selling it at Rs 2 crs. You have a gain of Rs 1 cr, which is called long-term capital gain. In certain assets, *long-term* may be used for assets held for more than one year, and in some assets, it may be for those held more than three years.

Calculating Taxable Capital Gain

To calculate the taxable capital gain, the inflation-adjusted value of the property is calculated using the government's inflation index. This means that if inflation in a year is 5%, then the government assumes the value of property is at least Rs 1.05 cr at the end of the year, and only sale proceeds above this amount are taxed.

Again, to simplify the discussion, assume inflation was at 5% annually for the last 10 years. By this logic, after an annual inflation of 5%, the property will get valued at approximately 1.63 cr after 10 years. Only the sale proceeds received above Rs 1.63 crs are taxable. The total sale proceeds, Rs 2 crs minus the inflation adjusted cost, Rs 1.63 cr, gives us Rs 0.37 cr. This, Rs 0.37 cr, is the amount on which the capital gains tax is levied. The capital gains tax is approximately 20%.

So 20% of Rs 0.37 crs gives us 7.4 lacs, which is the tax amount payable to the government.

Post Tax Income

Let us assume you are a senior corporate honcho, and in the same year, you received a bonus of Rs 1 cr. On this, you will have to pay a 30% income tax. The amount received in hand, post-tax, is approximately 70 lacs. So within the same year you received a gain from property of Rs 1 cr and salary bonus of Rs 1 cr in the case of property you paid a tax of Rs 7.4 lacs and in case of salary bonus you paid a tax of Rs 30 lacs! Every rupee lost in taxes is a rupee less for compounding.

To take this example further, let us assume you were holding shares for many years and finally sold them at a loss of Rs 10 lacs. You could net off the loss of Rs 10 lacs against the gain from the property of Rs 37 lacs and pay taxes only on the balance gain of Rs 27 lacs. In the case of capital gain, you have the provision of netting off loss against gain. This is not available in the case of income.

Let me share the case of Savita, 45 yrs. old. Savita had an investible surplus of Rs 100 lacs. She was risk-averse and wanted to place the funds in a 3-year bank deposit at 8 %. I mentioned that she could consider the alternative of placing the funds in a fixed maturity Plan holding 'AAA' bonds (type of debt Mutual fund) offering a yield of 7.75%.

She was surprised to learn, that in the case of fixed deposit even though she was considering cumulative options, she would have to pay income tax on the accrued interest each year. In a cumulative option, the principal invested, and interest earned are received at the end of the tenure of the FD. At 8% per annum, she would earn approx. Rs 24 lacs cumulative interest (pre-tax) after 3 years. But on the approx. Rs 8 lacs interest accrued each year, she would have to pay approx. Rs 2.4 lacs tax each year for each of the three years.

In the case of Fixed Maturity Plan she would receive a gain of approximately Rs 23.25 lacs at end of year three. Since gains from Mutual Funds are treated as capital gains, this would be adjusted for inflation before being taxed. Assume inflation was 5% for each of the three years. Inflated cost of investment of Rs 100 lacs is Rs 115 lacs and maturity value is Rs 123.25 lacs. Thus inflation adjusted 'taxable' gain is Rs 17.25 lacs. A capital gains tax of approx. 20% is applicable. Tax payable is Rs 3.45 lacs.

So after 3 years in case of Fixed deposit (@ 8%) investment, total tax paid is Rs 7.2 lacs and income in hand is Rs 16.8 lacs, whereas in case of the Fixed Maturity Plan (@ 7.75%), total tax paid is Rs 3.45 lacs and income in hand is Rs 19.8 lacs.

***

Over a 20 to 30-year journey of wealth creation, it makes a huge difference for investments to be compounded without leakage of income through taxes. This can be achieved through investment in shares, mutual funds, bonds, real estate etc. A significant difference between the wealthy and not so wealthy is the ownership of assets, which provides compounding benefit.

The wealthy receive a significant part of their earnings through capital gains. Capital gains are taxed at a much lower rate than income, leaving more money in hand to reinvest.

Chapter 10

Start Now

Every financial worry you want to banish and financial dream you want to achieve comes from taking tiny steps today that put you on a path toward your goals.

– Suze Orman

Ladies, please internalize, that you too can be wealthy! You do not need to earn in crores to be wealthy. You just need to save, invest and buy assets diligently for years to come.

Take the example of the Sharnas who earn Rs 40 lacs and spend Rs 30 lacs. So they are saving 25%

of their income. Now take the Mathurs who are earning Rs 80 lacs and spending Rs 70 lacs. Their saving rate is only 12.5%; half of that of the Sharnas. And considering their lifestyle cost is double that of the Sharnas they will have a very difficult time sustaining their lifestyle through retirement.

***

Michael Jackson was one of the highest paid singers & performers of his times. But when he died, Jackson was between $400 million and $500 million in debt. Much of Jackson's wealth went into the funding and upkeep of his famous Neverland Ranch. There are thousands of such examples; people who earned 'large' amounts of money but then went on 'larger' spending sprees and ended up in debt.

Being wealthy is not about achieving an absolute number or achieving a particular lifestyle. It is about building a net worth which can sustain one's chosen lifestyle for long periods, giving one the option to exercise various life choices. In a small Indian village, a person with a cemented house and a motorcycle parked outside, would be considered wealthy.

And in an Indian metropolis a person with a Rs 1 cr apartment would be considered middle class.

Start your wealth creation journey today. Journey, implies travelling from one place to another. So first define your starting point. Then fix your destination, your financial goal. Only then can you plan out your journey.

Step 1: Assess

Assess your present situation and calculate your net worth.

Assets (A)	Liabilities (L)
Property other than your home	
Employee Provident Fund	Loans
Bonds	Credit card bills
Mutual Funds	
Deposits	
Direct Equity	
Unit Linked Insurance policy	
Net worth = Total Assets (A) - Total Liabilities (B)	

Your Net Worth Should Be Positive

If it is not, you need to plan to reduce your liabilities and increase assets. Your assets may include jewellery, artefacts, etc. Anything of financial value is an asset. Liquidate some assets (investments) to pay off loans, particularly high-cost credit card debt and consumer loans. Ensure your assets are diversified and some assets are liquid (easily redeemable).

Step 2: Financial Plan

Start with a plan. Then articulate and define your financial goals. Your goals could be short term or long term. For example buying a house in 5 years' time or saving for a child's college education in 15 years' time. The financial goal needs to be defined in terms of time duration and approximate present value. So one could say that the goal is to buy an apartment in 5 years which costs approximately Rs 1 cr today. This will enable one to factor in the approximate price escalation over 5 years. So the target would be to have a corpus of Rs 1 cr plus estimated escalation by end of 5 years.

Plan a monthly budget so that savings and investible amounts are defined for each goal. Use online financial calculators or the services of a financial planner to assess the monthly investments needed to reach your goal. Your investment check should be the first check paid out of your salary account each month. Household and lifestyle expenses should be addressed out of the balance.

Step 3: Risk Profile

Risk profile is a measure or assessment of your risk-taking ability from a psychological point of view. Each of us has a different tolerance limit for volatility. A person's risk profile is independent of age or wealth accumulated. If a conservative person has a high exposure to equities, she will not be able to tolerate the valuation swings in her portfolio as the equity market goes through cycles.

For a portfolio to be sustainable over longer periods of time, it must be constructed as per the risk profile of the investor. Evaluate your opportunities and challenges. Start conversations on financial matters with your family and friends. Remember, the majority of the millionaires today are self-made.